Bridging The Gap Between The Music Department & The Pulpit

Rev. Jerome Bell

Forward By
Dr. Teresa Hairston

Bridging The Gap Between The Music Department & The Pulpit
by Rev. Jerome Bell

Printed in the United States of America

ISBN 1-59781-953-0

Unless otherwise indicated, all Scripture quotations are from the King James Version of the Bible.

Contact Information:
The Bell Group & Ministries
P.O. Box 5636
Capital Heights, MD 20791
(301) 390-1337
Bellgroup@aol.com

Editing by:
Ms. Bonita V. White

www.xulonpress.com

Bridge - a structure that spans and provides passage across an obstacle.

Webster's II New Riverside Dictionary

Bridge - a link, a device for connection

Microsoft Thesaurus

Gap - an opening as in a wall: cleft. An empty space.

Webster's II New Riverside Dictionary

Gap - a whole, a slit, an opening, a breach!

Microsoft Thesaurus

BRIDGING THE GAP BETWEEN
THE MUSIC DEPARTMENT & THE PULPIT
Rev. Jerome Bell

Forward by
Dr. Teresa Hairston
Gospel Today Magazine & The Gospel Heritage Foundation

To my two dear, darling cherubs!

Tramaine Ashley Bell

&

Jonathan Allen Bell

I sang to you as infants and its still one of the greatest
messages I've ever given you in song,

"Always remember Jesus, Jesus.
Always keep Him on your mind."

- Andrae Crouch

OPENING PRAYER

Dear Lord, please allow the reader to be receptive of this offering that you have given to provoke thought and aide in bringing together two entities that you have established for your glory. Open Minds and soften hearts as you allow this offering to penetrate and bring forth transformation. Touch and bless gifts all over again. Anoint afresh. Bless now each ministry and minister that desires to play an active roll in the process of Bridging the Gap Between The Music Department and the Pulpit as you intended. We thank you for your joy for it *is* the joy of the Lord that has become our strength. And we use that strength to give you praise, glory and honor. Help us today that we may better glorify you as we are edified and satan is horrified! In the precious, inexhaustible, matchless, name of Jesus, Amen.

FORWARD

When it comes to the "marriage" between musician and pastor, there is much to be considered. First and foremost, there must be a healthy respect for the other. Second, there must be a mutual contribution to a relationship that works for the growth of the ministry and the building of the Kingdom.

In this book, you will explore many aspects of history, both biblical and current, that impact the present-day church and its need to see pastors and musicians work in "concert."

Jerome Bell has served as a manager, agent, clinician and pastor. He has been "on the scene" and has certainly traversed "the circuit" of both music and ministry. He is well able to guide you through this sensitive area.

Read this book with an open heart and mind. Read it with a passion to learn, grow and implement new ideologies and strategies in your ministry. Read it and become a better steward of your gift and your relationship with your co-laborers in ministry. Finally, read it and be blessed!

Teresa Hairston

ACKNOWLEDGEMENTS:

First to the Almighty God! My Lord and Savior, Jesus Christ for His keeping power! And to the precious gift of the Holy Spirit for leading guiding and directing. Lord you ARE a keeper! Thank you!

There should be music playing in the background of these acknowledgements. They tell a story.

To my mom, Brenda Bell Williams. My mother's love of music definitely rubbed off on me. There was always music, always records. Whether there was company or not, we'd have music! And if we did have company, it *surely* meant music. That was also the beginning of my being "on stage!"

Like many, I, too, used the brush or the empty toilet paper holder or the empty paper towel holder as my microphone. And, for three minutes or so, whatever the length of the record, I was literally trans-formed to "the Artist!" That was the beginning of my knowledge of the power of music. After all, I had been Al Green, James Brown, and ALL of the Temptations. And you KNOW I'd even been Michael Jackson. Although, I must admit, I actually enjoyed being Jermaine even more! He always seemed a bit cooler and had lots of style. Though nothing ever became of it, I would often use the radiator as my piano. I played so hard. I really should be able to play the piano!

I sincerely thank my mother for all of that music and so much more. The first Gospel 45 I remember us having was "Oh Happy Day!" by Edwin Hawkins! That was in the late 60's. [Who could have ever thought that I would have the opportunity to work with Brother Edwin and the rest of The Hawkins Family. The Lord truly works in mysterious ways!] In the early 70s, Billy Preston's, "My Sweet Lord", along with the Queen of Soul, Aretha Franklin's awesomely timeless "Amazing Grace" album, which was recorded with the Southern California Community Choir and the late great Rev. James Cleveland at his church in Los Angeles permeated our airwaves. THAT album was definitely a favorite of my mom's. My brother, Jeffrey and I often awoke to "Amazing Grace" playing with the smell of bacon, potatoes, and scrambled eggs (unless it was scrambled eggs mixed with sausage), and toast on Saturday AND Sunday mornings! Aretha would be blasting as if the concert were coming from our living room! And it was serious church for the time of that recording. Thanks, Mom for planting the seeds and nurturing the plant! I love you!

Pastor Robert L. Walls, Sr., who has now gone on to be with the Lord, always kept me encouraged through whatever was going on! I remember not knowing exactly what I was going to do, but I knew I wanted to do something great! Pastor Walls always told me that I could and I would!

Pastor Walls told me I would be preaching at a time that I wasn't even attending Sunday School or Bible Study! And, it was such an honor to have preached my initial sermon and to have been licensed by Pastor Walls in **December 1994.**

Looking back, our relationship perhaps epitomizes the theme of this offering. I recall Pastor Walls allowing me to coordinate the choir's anniversary. I brought in drums, with a new drummer, Clarence Parks who had MORE drums than most regular kits (and that was NOT cool), a bass player, Quinton McCall who had a HUGE amp and DX6 for our organist to sit on top of the organ! By the looks of their faces, I thought the deacons and a few of our seniors were ready to throw me out for sure! It didn't feel as happy a time as I thought it should have felt as we came marching down the aisle with all of this instrumentation going on. But Pastor Walls stood up, smiled and clapped encouraging his young people and the rest became history! Today, New Macedonia Baptist Church has musical instrumentation all over the place! Not to mention that the guys I brought in to play that day became members of the church and now they are ALL PASTORS! [Look at God!] Pastor Walls was a true gem of a mentor. I miss him tremendously for his wise counsel and just for being Pastor Walls, on whom I could depend.

Another great influence in my life has been the incomparable **Tramaine Hawkins Richardson.** Being with Tramaine, I experienced ministry at all levels and from all sorts of perspectives. There were times that being on the road with Sister Tramaine meant 6:00 a.m. prayer, working the altar, sitting with souls counseling and tarrying for two and three hours after the service was over, etc. I had not done those kinds of things with any other artists. We traveled the globe with ministry. From Germany, France, London, the Caribbean, Canada, the U.S. and more. ALL for the purpose of ministry. Through Tramaine, I was embraced by many preachers and pastors. Tramaine comes from a family of ministry and they've become my family too! Traveling with this legend also gave me more insight into the need for music and ministry to work together as many times, I witnessed her concern that she would be in the "flow of the Spirit" to aid these various pastors achieve their vision of the service. Tramaine never just shows up to be "The Star!" She has been a great example of showing love to the people, such as the times she has stayed to sign autographs for the entire arena while other artists left to head off to the restaurant or other destinations. A trailblazer, as you know, Tramaine is just as gracious and supportive off stage as she is on stage and she is just as comfortable in the audience encouraging others as she is being cheered herself.

Richard Smallwood, My Lord! Another story all by itself. Let me tell you about Richard Lee. He ALWAYS said I'd be a PASTOR. I remember thinking, "… that doesn't even make sense… I'm not even preaching." I thought Richard was WAY off with that one! Needless to say he was too happy at my trial sermon which came about 6 or 7 years after he had proclaimed that. The night of the trial sermon, I thought that was it. Richard pointed out that I was finally on my way to pastoring. I couldn't believe he said that to me! It has come to pass. So, I started calling him a prophet.

I went on one date with Richard Smallwood and The Smallwood Singers in 1981 to Houston, Texas to celebrate the Southeast Inspirational Choir's Anniversary. They had an awesome song, "My Liberty!" that I was the first to play on the radio in the D.C. area so it was cool to celebrate with them. We thought the soloist would be a plus-sized, older woman with big hair - and - to our surprise - it was our introduction to Yolanda Adams! Wrong description!

A couple of years after that Richard asked me to go on an engagement with The Smallwood singers as Road Manager and I thought I was just going on THAT engagement. I didn't know my road managing would continue for nearly 19 years! Needless to say, I saw and learned a lot by being on the road with Richard and The Smallwood Singers and met a lot of people, many of whom have become dear friends to this day. Thanks a lot, Rich! It is amazing how people can see in you what you may not see in yourself!

Shirley Ables Starks, one of the greatest gospel artists ever known. Though she is in the Gospel Music Hall of Fame, she never got the national acclaim she deserved (to me). Not only did Shirley give me a boatload of singing and directing experiences and opportunities with various choirs and groups, but she was the one who took me to meet Madame Lucille Banks Robinson Miller at WYCB Radio. As only the second female radio announcer in the Washington, DC area, Madame Miller was a major pioneer and had lots of clout. I became Madame Miller's secretary, the station receptionist, radio personality, and traffic manager. At one point, I was doing all of that all at the same time! It was while I was at WYCB that I began to meet many of gospel's foremost recording artists, preachers and personalities of all genres of entertainment, from the late Rev. James Cleveland, The Barrett Sisters, the late Mother Mattie Moss Clark, The Clark Sisters, The Hawkins Family, Andrae Crouch to Stevie Wonder and The Jones Girls….even Cat woman, Eartha Kit! All because SHIRLEY ABLES took me down there! Thanks again, Mother Shirley!

Bonita V. White - O my good Lord! What history. Thank you for the encouragement, inspiration, and support through the years! Even the little nuggets of wisdom and direction you would offer back in the day when I worked at the radio station before we needed to dial the area code and continue to offer even now. I just thank you for being there! You are a true gem. I am blessed to be able to call on you. You always always bring something special to the table.

To those who help to keep it all together at MFCC: Deacon Tony and Sis. Richelle James, Bro. Reggie and Sis. Jackie Allen,

Elder Richard Toye, Rev. Eric and Lady Phyllis Cooper, Evelyn Ford, Helen "Queen" Fielding, Tonita LaTrice, Darryl and Cherlyn Guinyard, and ALL of The Maryland Family Christian Center!

To Pastor Patrick and Lady Priscilla Walker and The New Macedonia Baptist Church family, Dr. Teresa Hairston, an awesome woman of God and a great inspiration of helping others to the understanding the necessity of "Business IN Ministry". She does it with such style and grace. I've always been impressed and inspired.

To Evangelist Dorinda Clark Cole - love you madly, and I thank Elder Greg Cole too for allowing Dorinda to be our friend! Rev. Daniel Harrison, Elder Elmer E. Cleveland who did our first revival at MFCC (and we didn't have music at all! Bishop Ernestine Cleveland Reems Dickerson, I'll never forget that sermon, "The Lord Hath Need of Thee."

To Angela D. Bell - we did two great things! We're connected forever.

To the Queen of Gospel, Albertina Walker, Bishop Michael and Lady Sheila Kelsey, Dr. Bobby Jones, Oprah Winfrey for the life-changing Legends Weekend Experience and so much more inspiration! God CAN dream a bigger dream for you than you can for yourself. I appreciate you.

To Carla Reed, Dr. Carla Bowens, Aldonia Hardy, Pastor Donnie McClurkin, Bishop Paul S. Morton, Bishop Albert Jamison, Pastor Shirley Caesar, Bishop Alfred and Evangelist Susie Owens, Mother Shirley M. K. Berkeley, The Heaven 1580 crew, Cathy Hughes, Jeffmajors Graham, Karen Jackson, Lynda Nix! Sabrina Madison, VISION, Overseer Lanier Twyman, Bryant Jeffrey Pugh, Jonathan DuBose - my son has a great name, keep expecting the unexpected! To Joel Bryant - the years, the mileage, the experiences - Joel Smith, Jeff Davis, Steven Ford, Patrick Lundy, Rick & Lorree Slye, Curtis King, Bishop Andrew Merritt, Wanda Grant, Carla Townsend, Alvin & Priscilla (CeCe Winans) Love, Pastor Keith Reid, Dr. Creflo Dollar, Patrick Henderson, Pastor Thomas Wiley, BeBe Winans, Pastors Grainger & Joanne Browning, Bishop Eddie Long - what an experience preaching there! Apostle Betty Peebles, Pastor Keith and Lady Donita Martin, Mother Carolyn Harrison, Pastor James Sturdivant, Wesley Boyd, Jackie Ruffin, Lisa Burroughs Allen,

Carolene Hatchet, Darlene Simmons, Dottie Jones, Vanessa Bell Armstrong, Vicki Winans, Tracy Martin and to those that have gone on: my grandmother, the late Gladys Bell, Howard Sanders, who gave me that first radio job! Lucille Banks Robinson Miller - whew! Deacon Joseph Harrison, Donn Edwards Miller, Forest McCain and Tim Linzy.

And, finally to my neighbors, the lady at the bank, the grocery store clerk, the mechanics that keep the car in warranty, and YOU for reading all of this!

May the Lord continue to bless, keep, and use you all!

THIS IS MY STORY

Over the past 25 years (or more), I've been a choir member, choir founder, choir director, production coordinator, radio announcer, radio program director, revival sponsor, revival evangelist, artist road manager, artist manager, artist booking agent, and now I pastor The Maryland Family Christian Center. It continues to be an awesome journey. I've gone from being the ear for the pastor to express desire for a musician to being the pastor with a desire for a good musician! Whew! I've even had to interview musicians and pastors for various events and occasions, as well as for radio broadcasts. I've seen the focus of many (good and bad) as well as the attitudes (good and bad). I've experienced more lessons from being back stage, on the road, and as a part of the "crew" than most colleges would have time to hold class for.

Now that I sit in the seat of the pastor, it is all the more clear. "What a revelation!", I thought when the Holy Spirit gave me this assignment. I recall standing on stage with about 4,000 people in the audience waiting for the event to begin. The event being, "A Tribute to Tramaine Hawkins", which literally took the Pastor, The Music Department to and everyone else to work together to prepare the brand new sanctuary. We were all slinging chairs that had just come in straight out of the box and just in time for The Tribute. We were making last minute final touches to the sanctuary, the setting, the dressing rooms for the many artists to arrive, checking out things in the lobby of the church, the bathrooms, etc. You name it! We were in it and on it, together!

Drs. T. L. Lowery and Steven Lowery, Pastors of The National Church of God, the host church for The Tribute, made themselves available to pray, attend meetings, and to be involved in any way necessary to ensure the success of the event. The Pastors were concerned about the instrumentation requirements, the sound, the seating, the food, the transportation... just everything! I thought, "WOW!!!....This is different and how awesome it would be if this level of interest and concern shown by these pastors were the norm for our churches and that the musical staff could reciprocate by showing as much concern for events spearheaded by the pastors, such as the revivals, conferences and other meetings. (By the way, the pastors at National were also planning for one of the biggest revivals they had ever had to be held the following week, which was a huge success. I believe it was due in great part to the spirit that was left in the house from the Tribute to Tramaine that preceded!)

Throughout all of my experiences, THIS I know, when the pastor and the musician are on one accord, the rest becomes easy. For the gate is well kept! Now, let's get it on!

OBSERVATIONS

Have you ever been in a service and the Spirit of the Lord was moving, working things out and you could just see people being freed up, encouraged, and motivated by the power of God to just go on? I mean HIGH PRAISE is going on! You would think that the hierarchy of the physical church would be for this! You would think that there would be total support of and sensitivity to this move occurring ... yet, you become immediately disappointed by a gesture that shows you otherwise. This lack of support can come from either side of the spectrum we're discussing. When the support is not there from one side or the other (and I have seen it happen both ways) the rest of the body ends up suffering or denied. An insensible and indefensible lack. Lack many times in the sense that whatever it is that they think they have, they have only scratched the surface of what was really in store for the whole body to receive, however because of the hierarchy discord... WE missed it! It was shut down! If we had these understandings, I'm certain we'd all be frustrated. Yes, we can see how far we've come, but realizing how much farther we could be if there had been obedience, reverence, sensitivity, and understanding in the house ought to provoke us to not make these same mistakes again and increase our desire to redeem the time! We want the house to be blessed. We're talking about the Lord's house. Blessing His house will bless your house!

I've been afforded the pleasure to work with several luminaries and entities in the Gospel Music industry in myriad capacities out front and behind the scenes in management, road management, touring, hosting, coordinating, producing, radio and television, the "Conference Boom" and other areas. I call it the "Conference Boom" because some remember when there were no "conferences" and the only conventions were the Thomas A. Dorsey Convention of Choirs and Choruses and then the James Cleveland Gospel Music Workshop of America. Today, though, these remain forerunners and forces to reckon with, there are conferences to fill the complete calendar of the year. Seems like everyone has a conference!

Some of those with whom I have worked and traveled and have given me the opportunity to be "involved" in a very intricate way and have facilitated these observations are Tramaine Hawkins, Richard Smallwood & The Smallwood Singers, and later Richard Smallwood and Vision, Vanessa Bell Armstrong, Vickie Winans, Jonathan DuBose, Kim Burrell, The Clark Sisters, The Edwin Hawkins Music & Arts Seminar, the "Queen" of Gospel, Albertina Walker, BET, Dr. Bobby Jones Gospel, various radio stations, and of course, The Gospel Music Workshop of America, just to name a few. Through my works and travels with these and other ministries (including churches), I've seen lots of hindrances of the "work." I've seen a lot of positives too, but, of course, it's the negative things that seem to weigh us down! There's nothing like knowing what things COULD be if folk would have only followed directions! It's about the work! Winning souls for the Kingdom of God! I've seen hindrances firsthand of some of the greatest, forced into situations and circumstances that were just unnecessary. Their names and likenesses have been used, misdirected, talents and gifts treated without reverence. There were even times that you could say that their names and likenesses were not used sufficiently or there were missed opportunities to allow ministry to flow or times when things could have been done in a more effective way for the cause of Christ. It's about the "work!" After the event or "gig" was over, I'd just wonder "what was that all about?" Particularly if no one discusses souls being saved, people being empowered, encouraged, motivated. Or, if there were no discussions or hopes of deliverance, joy, peace, and all the things that we ought to be hopeful and praying for. What was the true bottom line to the event, the service, the ministry? Was it another time of financial opportunity where all the success is weighed solely on the fact that the offering or ticket sales was more than enough if enough at all to just pay the bills. Now, we must be clear and understand that "bill paying" is a very important part of the ministry as well! Who's in charge now? Is this musical/event without a pastoral covering? Is it all business and no ministry? What's going on? Who follows up for the praise report? Should there be a praise report? Don't we need to have clarity on the intention that we may take the responsibility to seek a praise report? Pastor? Musician? CEO? Where are we? What are we doing? We sure had a good time and the music and the preaching was great though!! This mentality is so prevalent IN the church. We see those seeking to have a polished service from start to finish, flowing well for television, the tapes are rolling, etc. We've got make up artists, sound crews, etc. for some Sunday morning worship services these days you know, but is it really clear that we desire to build the Kingdom of God or are we building little kingdoms for our ourselves. How much production is too much production? We've got to be careful here, because some don't think production should be brought in to the church. Some argue that there needs to be more production in the church. I think that much of that mindset has to do with the fact there needs to be more structure in the church. In some cases structure period as opposed to freelance church! Not to be stiff or deny the move of the Holy Spirit to alter the change of the program. If there were no structure, you couldn't tell if there was a change! There's nothing wrong with excellence. Striving for excellence and a better way is what it's all about. The pulpit and the music department lead the way in that strive. Effective ways to get the "work" done! God's got to be first and stronger relationships will help to get the job done. I pray, hope, and trust that there would be a sharing, an outpouring of information and wealth certainly coupled with fervent prayer that we would be endowed with the strength and tools to do a better job when it comes to winning souls for the kingdom of God... not just exchanging members. You know the "I used to go to this church, now I go to this church." THAT doesn't indicate that any new members have been brought to the kingdom. Those would be transfers! It is time that we become real fishers of men and attract those that don't come from anybody's church. That's also going to take the coming down of egos, schisms, and isms, and the realization (once again) that the Kingdom of God is bigger than your church AND your denomination. *The body hath many members.* There's a place for all the talents He blesses us with. Nothing replaces the "head." Anything with two heads is a monster! So we're not saying that the Pastor and the Chief musician are BOTH heads of the church, we're saying a tighter union of the two will make way for a more effective approach at winning souls for the kingdom of God. The sister over in the alto section who does not sing lead needs to be appreciated just at the one that's been dubbed the "star soprano lead singer." Imagine the director having his hands give a direction and nothing happens! Embarrassing! Oh yeah, we've seen that happen, too. Without the choir, the director and all of his or her direction is unnecessary. Equally, those sharing the roster with the pastor or the preacher of the hour ought to be his or her number one backers...AND the choir ought to be right there with the preachers and the preachers ought to be right there with the choir! Can you imagine how awesome that service would be? If the pulpit got with the choir, it would lead the congregation to get with the choir. If the choir got with the pulpit, it would also lead the congregation to get with the message as well. But, if the two are not working in tandem for the purpose of the work, the intention is missed... again. The Kingdom of God is the Kingdom of God! That's it! Now to get that and to see the repeated misuse of talents and positions is just unbearable. There is so much more work that can be done if we would just realize who we are, what we already have, and not forget the purpose. I often repeat from the pulpit at The Maryland Family Christian where I pastor, "In the beginning, God!" That's straight from Genesis 1:1.

The beginning of any book will basically tell you what the book is about. For example: "Once upon a time there lived a girl named Ashley", or "It was a lonely, dark and sultry night..." You generally get the scene or focal point at the very beginning. Well, the Bible gives us, "In the beginning, GOD!" Letting us know that this thing is about God, not us. The Bible even goes further, as I was so graciously reminded by former James Cleveland Singer and sweetheart to the Kingdom, Evangelist and First Lady, Betty Griffin Keller, "We didn't even show up for twenty six verses thereafter!" So you see, God was working on many things before He even got to us! And, even after He got to us in verse twenty-six, it STILL ain't about us. The trees, bees, birds, fish, etc., all came before us. The awesomeness of our being, though, is that through all of His creations we are the ones to whom He gave dominion. He handed responsibility to us after all he had done. We, too, are the only ones in whom He breathed His own breath. We are truly blessed from our beginning. He instructs us to praise Him if we have this same breath. And, we do! So, if we don't praise Him, we are being disobedient. We are the only creation of the creator that does not follow directions. The birds are not trying to be trees, the fish are not trying to be the fowl of the air. We are intended to be the praisers. We must praise. Some say, the praises we send up become noticeable to other beings and creatures too....meaning that if you have a spider in your church or home and you've got some praises going up, the spider gets it! It follows then that, at the coliseum, stadium, concert hall or whatever the venue, the rats can tell the difference between a gospel concert vis-a-vis the events of the world. Great thought, huh?

This we KNOW, the Lord inhabits the praises of His people and there is power, much power in praising the Lord. Yes, praises serve as a weapon of which we are consistently reminded throughout Scripture. It seems that because of this very fact, however, we experience suppression and other tactics of the enemy, even in ministry, which hinder or attempt to prevent us from giving the Lord praise continuously - even in times of difficulty. Knowing that there is historic and Biblical separation between the music department and the pulpit, imagine the power that comes to the house when these two lead the way in praises! Yes, we have talents, technology, beauty, looks, outfits, etc. But, the sincerity of defined, strong, uninhibited, aggressive, knowledgeable, secure leadership is the very area where the kingdom building process suffers. This is the very topic of this reading. If the two parties of the relationship responsible of leading us in the worship experience were clear, really clear, there'd be no stopping!

THE CO-MISSION

Without a doubt, there is a necessity for ministries to understand the need to develop a more cohesive relationship between the pulpit and the music department. Interestingly enough, many preachers are "frustrated singers" and or musicians anyway. Some are even very qualified to handle all three of the positions. Let's face the reality: Preachers LIKE to hang out with musicians! With "stars", celebrities and the like. Do musicians feel the same way? Hmmmmmm? Certainly, music is a ministry which should be offered to win souls for the Kingdom of God. Music does and can have its ministerial effect with even more intensity if all members of The Body are working together.

Following the Scripture:

For as the body is one and hath many members, and all the members of that one body, being many, are one body: so also is Christ.

- I Corinthians 12

Therefore, when these two departments have understanding and unity amongst themselves, the Great Commission (emphasis on CO-mission) is more successfully accomplished. Taking a look at where we are now, we realize that there are more "Word" and "Empowerment" conferences than ever before. Most of these conferences seek nationally and internationally known artists to serve as psalmists to attract

29

more delegates. This is a clear sign of the need for unity between the two gifts to the Body. Scripturally and practically speaking many of today's ministries have evidenced growth and thrived because they possess a music department that is capable of attracting new visitors and converts that the preached word does not. Most often the stage for such life-changing events is set by music ministers who have been instrumental in the coordination of the event.

It is important to understand that to many people, the sense of who the church really is, is dictated by these two departments and how they work together. When there is an issue between these two departments, it is church news and fodder for the proverbial grape vine. Everybody really wants to know what's going on. As in any case, maintaining a relationship requires continual work. Constant commitment is key. Keep it fresh. The courting never ends. The lines of communication must remain open directly between the two. All too often, that is not the case with music ministry and the ministry of the Word. Nonetheless, there must be a genuine love for the job on behalf of both or all parties. We must also understand the true meaning of love.

Charity suffereth long, and is kind; charity envieth not; charity vaunteth not itself, is not puffed up, Doth not behave itself unseemly, seeketh not her own, is not easily provoked, thinketh no evil; Rejoiceth not in iniquity, but rejoiceth in the truth; Beareth all things, believeth all things, hopeth all things, endureth all things. Charity never faileth

I Corinthians 13:4-8a

As you can see, this commitment is not for wimps. "Charity suffereth long..." It requires covering, not vaunting oneself or behaving unseemly leaving the ego at the door, not being the proud peacock - recognizing the gift comes from the Creator and not over glorifying the creature.

And, also important all parties should be endowed and display the fruit of the spirit for the good of the Body and, in the best interest of accomplishing the mission of winning souls for Christ.

Galatians 5:22 says:

But the fruit of the Spirit is love, joy, peace, longsuffering, gentleness, goodness, faith. Meekness, temperance: against such there is no law.

Both music ministry and ministry of the Word are scriptural based, God-ordained positions. Both must be executed with love, evidencing the commitment to fulfill the Great Commission. Working together serves as an excellent example o the congre- gation at large of the love that exists between the two ministries and can serve as the model for other auxiliaries to follow. Of course, the pastor ALWAYS wants to be part of the positive example and so ought the minister of music. Providing a Christ-like example also shows that the positions go beyond just the gifts, the abilities and talents of the musicians' staff and pulpit. It exemplifies love for the ministry and for the Body of Christ. Remember, the greatest of these is love.

After the courtship, interview and hiring process, unfortunately, the direct line between the music department and the pulpit often becomes filtered and tainted. This phenomenon can be attributed to a variety of factors all of which are against Biblical principles. Factors such as egotism, envy, haughtiness, self-righteousness. Open communication and recognition of the CO-mission will assist in several areas. Further, recognition of the fact that all parties are being observed at all times, means people are watching how the ministers interact with each other throughout the service (i.e., the chemistry or conflict) and how they complement one another in AND outside of the church. It is a proven fact that visitors like to know if they are going to hear good, sound preaching, as well as good music, at least a good song! Both should perpetuate excellence in ministry and leave the visitor member with a sense of reverence to both. Not to mention the need for consistence in the relationship between the music department and the minister, so that the membership will feel comfortable and confident in inviting others to visit and join. Again, we have to remember that the ENTIRE point of it ALL is to win souls for the Kingdom of God!

And here's a NEWSFLASH for you:
The Kingdom of God is bigger than *your* church!

We are clear that nothing replaces The Word of God! Reality also lets us know that if we are to grow the Kingdom of God down here before His return, then we have to do this by any means necessary. For we all have a role to play and there's enough work for all of us to do. "For we are workers together in Christ...."

Working together allows us to share in the victories together! When one has a victory, the Body has the victory. The accomplishment of one is the accomplishment of all:

And whether one member suffer, all the members suffer with it; or one Ember be honored all the members rejoice with it.
- I Corinthians 12:26

Primarily, we are prepared and are already made aware that the attraction of most churches is going to be the preacher and the musicianship. The sermons, the songs, the music of the church, the form and style of praise and the ability to join in, be accepted, etc., represent the foundation for growth. Further, working together demonstrates the results of addressing structure and testifies to the benefit which derives from operating within scriptural guidelines:

Let all things be done decently and in order.
- I Corinthians 14:40

THE LEVITES AND THE PRIESTS

Let us consider the origin of these offices as recorded in the Scriptures which serve as our earliest role models in terms of form and function. Throughout the books of Exodus and Numbers, you see the trials, tribulations of the Levites and Priests and scriptural descriptions as to how they should function. This is a great start to obtaining an understanding as to how it used to be and how it differs today. Surely, there is a need for help and clarity in understanding the functions and the relationships if we truly desire to be scriptural in our approach to dealing with music department and the pulpit. Of course we do not live in that time and some of those duties are no longer required, but the mindset of the office should remain the same. There was nothing wrong with the original foundation of the office, we just had to adapt some of the principles to contemporary ties. By analogy, it is like the typewriter and the computer. There was nothing wrong with the typewriter, we just upgraded with technology, but we kept the same keypad for the computer.

Musicians, as Levites, were originally regarded as servants. Note, that in the day of the Levite, we were also in the day of Priest, High Priest and Chief Levite. The Levites, descendants of Levi, and then there were those who were the sons of Aaron. Their duties were quite extensive. They served as assistants to the Priest in the ownership of Israel and led the people in worship and confession. They were often charged with the responsibility of the priesthood, took care of the tabernacle and the temple, performed menial duties, served as doorkeepers, members of the temple orchestra and had administrative duties as well. In the day of the tabernacle, before the use of the Temples, the Levites would transport is and its furniture during the daytime hours when the camp would be moved from place to place. The Levites also prepared and baked the show bread and did whatever was necessary in connection with the sacrifices for the ceremonies. They also examined the lepers for the sake of the law and went as far as to help the priest to slaughter and skin the animals for sacrifice. So you see, musicians and singers could not just show up and sing or play. They were a part of the set up. Be involved.

There were known to be four (4) classes of Levites: 1) assistants to priests in the work of the sanctuary; 2) judges and scribes; 3) gatekeepers and 4) musicians. Through all of their experiences and tasks, it is no wonder that they had such a faith in the power of the Lord. It is often stated that the Lord knew that the Levites at times had more of "the Heart of God" than the very priests.

Also note that many priests held positions because of heredity, not necessarily because of a calling, while the Levites were given a special place by the Lord because of the honor they extended to Him. The Levites were the first to show God honor and feel guilty for their actions (repentance) in the time that Moses had gone up into the mountains to hear from the Lord. You remember the story the people began to grow weary and created gods of their own. They became festive and sinful. Upon Moses' return, however, even in their guilty state, when he had called for those who were on the Lord's side, the Levites were the first to rally to his side. Levites have always been on the front line. Even today, when it is time for testimony, time for someone to speak and testify to the goodness of the Lord, we witness our Levites, our singers and musicians, administrators and officers leading the way, extolling the congregation and facilitating their understanding and participation. There is so much more to it than just singing and playing. There is a blessing in participation! This also helps to bridge the gap! It is not as simple and easy as "I just play for the services on 2nd and 4th Sundays and do two rehearsals", as some Levites of today protest all to be necessary. If those are the only Sundays you serve or when ever you serve. Your whole heart ought to be in those services. You can not be one who simply chooses to watch soap operas, shop, hang out, exempt themselves from BIBLE STUDY, administrative concerns, preparation of today's temples, etc. The position of the Levites of old entailed much, much more. Again, they were right on the front line of ministry! Needless to say, pulpit members ought not to perceive sharing the front line as intimidation, but ought to accept such assistance as it is helpful for the ministry and it is scriptural. Both parties must understand who gives direction and be sensitive to the Holy Spirit. The Levite, however, is always under subjection to the priest, i.e., the Pastor. This being the case, know that when the struggle arises, it is also that the enemy has come into the camp. We will discuss that later! Stay in the flow and remember, worship is a lifestyle!

The Lord loved the Levites very much and looked out for them, just as he had the priests. For the Levites were given 48 cities, received tithes due God from the first fruits of the fields the flocks and hears. These were first fruits even of the first born and certain portions of peoples' sacrificial offerings. Of these tithes the Levites would then give tithes to the priests. Giving honor to the musicians and singers is well in order. I recall when I began to really get this many years ago and I would give honor to the musicians, the choir and singers as I would give honor to God, the Holy Spirit, the pastor ...you know the protocol. People would often ask me why?

Everyone involved in these positions should read the entire books of Exodus and Numbers, among others that specifically address the duties of these offices. Both books of the Bible are very valuable pieces to the commitment puzzle and will show that this literary offering is merely a reiteration! Lots of misconceptions exist because of the lack of knowledge - including the still taboo subject about PAYING MUSICIANS. It's in there! This could also squash any feelings that the musicians should never make more than the minister. Not saying that should be a rule, but, the fact is in some churches, it is explicitly stated, "Make sure that the singers don't get more money than the church!" Make no mistake about it, no one will EVER have more than "The Church", regardless of what is received in the offering. The church is the bride of the Lord. She will always be well taken care of. The Lord is coming back for His bride!

I was literally hit with "The Rule" once when I had produced a musical for a church's Building Fund. The musicians and minstrels came to pour out their hearts, even agreeing to come without contract or set fees (Hallelujah to that!) and the offering was good, very good, in fact, for the church AND the musicians. Not to mention that several groups were sharing the offering for the musical guests and all of them also participated in the giving process. But, because that basket had more in it than the Church's basket, I heard "The Rule" with my own ears! I could not believe what I was hearing. It was one of the most heart-wrenching experiences I had ever had working in the church. Was it greed? Did it have merit! I just could not see nor understand such a position when "the house" had truly been blessed spiritually AND financially! In fact, the offering which was lifted was the direct result of the ministry of those Levites. They went to battle in song! As in the Scriptures, there were times when the Levites were given what to do in battle when the priests did not know. The anointing was in the room! Healing and deliverance took place through the preached word in song. But with the mindset of that particular pastor in enunciating "The Rule", how could the next person be encouraged to use his relationships to bring music ministry into the church?

Despite the fact that the pastor holds the ultimate responsibility for the success or failure, however it goes, we must understand that every good idea or proper thing to do, does not emanate exclusively from the pastor. To hold the pastor accountable for everything that transpires is not necessarily fair. But, under the logical principles of accountability, the church has a pastor and when something goes wrong people are looking for the pastor and the pastor knows this. When operating cohesively, bridging that gap, the focus ought to be what is best for the Body of Christ, the folks who come to the church house for something from God. With the mindset that "no matter what, we are not going to leave the pastor standing alone! Pastor, we've got your back!", there has to be human concern. Those concerns ought to be shared. In New Testament ties, both Levites and priests presided in an attempt to bring back the warmth and human concern. (See John 1). This does not remove the pastor from accountability nor responsibility, but perhaps provides him or her to receive the "help." As pastors, we often pray and ask for help and when it comes we kill the spirit of "help" with our own agendas. Remember Abraham? Let Sarah help!

IN ORDER TO FORM A MORE PERFECT UNION

The Minister of Music and Minister of the Word must spend time together and commune together. They must get to know one another as in any other relationship. The musician needs to be informed of the vision, allowed to ask questions and engage in dialogue to get full understanding. After all, the Scripture says, "in all thy getting get understanding", If this were done, it would enable a context or frame of reference for expectations to be enunciated and measured. Meanwhile, the pastor or minister ought to be open and receptive to the Minister of Music and be capable of listening and getting to know the musician not just making him/her an employee of the ministry. Identifying mutual ground, finding out their dreams, vision and exploring ways in which the ministry can assist. *Build the people and the people will build the church!* Perpetuate earnest enhancement. This also builds loyalty and lifelong relationship. Be in it for the long run. Yes, we are all open to hurt and disappointment that comes with the territory, but at least there would be a point of reference and an opportunity to review direction as director, intent and vision would have been made clear. Therefore, any difference would be immediately recognized by either party. When there is structure and commitment to structure, we can evaluate ourselves. O yes, we know when we are out of order.

Bishop Andrew Merritt of The Straight Gate Church in Detroit, Michigan, offers, "The fact of the matter is the two departments belong together!" I met Bishop Merritt while on the road with Richard Smallwood. We were all very immediately impressed by his obvious love and care about the music and ministry or should I say the ministry and the music? It was clear that he had been involved in every aspect, from sound equipment to musical equipment and per- haps even to wardrobe, since he is such a meticulous dresser him- self). Bishop Merritt was very concerned that things went well with the music and its presentation for purposes of presenting excellence in ministry. Unfortunately, that level of concern remains a rarity with most pastors. THIS pastor (Bishop Merritt) stayed for the entire sound check, asked if everything was all right, then left, changed his outfit and returned like the rest of us. Most pastors just show up for "the gig" and have somebody else involved in that area. Not that Bishop Merritt would not or could not delegate, as he clearly had others working, the point is that he was just concerned. It was also evident that Bishop Merritt simply loves music. Straight Gate has a full recording studio at the church that was built with assistance by Fred Hammond! Now, this is not everybody's church, for sure! All churches do not have the budget for such, of course. Nor do most churches have such luminaries to assist, but, all ought to have the spirit of unity and be desirous of excellence as they work well in the present level. The increase will come.

Bishop Merritt further stated in our conversation that the Shepherd MUST oversee the operation of the music department and absolutely be involved. It would be foolish to just let them loose. When things get out of control or trouble starts just as in any other relationship - a communication breakdown is usually a root cause. Bishop Merritt confesses that his love for music was developed and nurtured at an early age by his grandmother. He grew up with many of the gospel giants and legends, such as Mahalia Jackson. The Harmonizing Four, etc., and like many, he also has a love for country and other music genres, but his heart is with gospel music. The Bishop added that the lyrics in country music are good stories, but unlike gospel, country music has no soul to reach the soul. Of course, in most cases, the African-American singer is able to deliver a more soulful sound because of the experiences of failure and victory, hope and faith and just a good, old-fashioned testimony of the journey.

The music industry can be creative, intelligent, diverse, etc., "But I am responsible", says Bishop Merritt. I totally agree. This is a major point for pastors and musicians to understand when it comes to his or her role of understanding the pastor's input in the music department. And, if the pastor does not get it or has not read this, the musician has a new challenge of relaying the importance of this message. The pastor IS the gift of the house. All must understand that the musician possesses gifts, the ability to play, sing, direct, compose orchestrate, even administrative in some cases. He or she may even possess a mesmerizing or magnetic personality. In any case, the musician must understand that he/she is subject to the leadership of the pastor. Anything contrary to that understanding would resemble the whole story as to why Lucifer was thrown out of Heaven. It was never intended for the musician to reign on his or her own or reign at all! Bring it together and watch it work. Go eat and talk. We all love that!

Scripturally, music was created to praise God, it was used to soothe, to prepare atmosphere, and certainly to give Him praise. The purpose of its creation was ALL about God! Though the intentions were defined, like any job or opportunity when any part or party goes outside of the intent there is trouble. Keep the communication going. Don't get to the point where you feel it is unnecessary to communicate. Even with skilled, anointed creative people. This, too, was Lucifer in the beginning. Though he played himself, he got to feeling himself. Not saying that you should not be confident about your gift. Remember however, it is not about you! You are blessed even with creativity to be a blessing to others. The creativity should be continuously cultivated, nurtured, appreciated given clear direction as to expectation. Not hindered, rejected nor allowed to be unsupervised. Prayerfully, enhancement, support and encouragement will also create an attitude of gratitude, loyalty, responsibility and priority to the ministry. At least the lines of communication would be open! This means to discuss whatever needs to be discussed. There is even a proper way to leave or move on. Amen, somebody! This would be clearly evident when dealing with a musician who really desires to be in the will of the Lord and just be "correct." Of course, I know some pastors are saying, "Oh yeah?"

Consider too both sides of this reading, some musicians are saying, "Wow, I should have been more subjective, even more inquisitive". There are just too many pastors who don't get this subject as well as musicians. You both have to understand. Occasionally, just ASK, "What can I do to make it better?" There doesn't have to be anything wrong for this to be a fair question. We ought to be constantly concerned about improvement. The bottom line is the necessity for more understanding between both parties. That is, not just understanding the duties of the person, but the person who is doing the duties. The courting never stops. With a richer understanding of each other's roles and duties, it becomes less likely for one to feel that he or she is being taken for granted. Face it. The reality is that some are merely guarding their gifts and talents from being taken advantage of, as some are on the defense to protect the church and not "give away the store". Many times, the defense mechanism kicks in due to previous experience. That, too, should be communicated to prevent tainting the new relationship with things that went wrong in the old one. Yes, we are still talking about the pulpit and the musician, but, again, these are the same principles that ensure healthy relationships of any kind. It's nothing new that folk have a tendency to bring luggage from a previous relationship to a new one. As undesirable, inadvisable and downright wrong as it may be, it happens. And, when that behavior or action is dealt with directly, it helps to facilitate the new path, opportunity and place that most desire. I mean, nobody wants to continually operate in hostile territory. And, there is no way to be imbued in such negativity and be creative and cooperative, too! Neither will take advantage of the other and each will respect the other's calling and desire of the other, and thus have a mind to help and *be* a help to serve the Body and be focused solely on being served. Not a mind of intimidation, discord, inferiority, or other mood or spirit of contradiction that leads to destruction or the musician/pastor-train wreck!

Once while ministering with the legendary Tramaine Hawkins, she pointed out to the singers that they have to be excited and skillful simultaneously. Their joy, by expression and presentation, should become contagious. The congregation or the audience would catch on. And at the same time, if they were operating in the opposite manner, they would catch on to that too. She went on to say, "support the lead vocalist, support the pastor or the preacher or who ever is ministering. Make it an inclusive time of celebration of the goodness of the Lord!" As she was going forward with that lesson, I was like, "Where's a pen? I must write this down. This is good information." The pastor was excited too, because he saw Tramaine instructing his cheerleaders. Yes, this is the gap being bridged at its finest. I guarantee you that as the pastor sees the singers/musicians backing him up in such a way and preparing the way for him or her to minister, his level of appreciation will surely increase. I've seen that love increase to the point where the pastor of one of our country's finest ministries even provided for the choir to have its own banquet at a banquet hall. Where the banquet was exclusively for them! THAT is showing love and appreciation. Value each other! You're both valuable to the process of winning souls for the kingdom of God. Be valuable and valu - able....i.e., be able to value!

LET THE MUSIC MOVE YOU!

We've been doing it for years. History shows we move as a people and we move with music! All ethnicities may have their own style, but the power of music's ability is exemplified by them all. People have protested, marched to the beat of their own drums and music. We exercise, drive our cars, clean our homes, even make love with music as a prerequisite! I mean when you are planning a romantic dinner with your spouse with candles it is not the music of Shirley Caesar or Mahalia Jackson that you have in mind. Luther Vandross, a little or Anita [Baker] is what sets it off. Even Babyface! I remember at the radio station when we would cut commercials, the client would often ask for certain music to depict the right feeling for the commercial. We had to do many a commercial over because it had the wrong music, the wrong feeling, the wrong mood because of the music. Music sets the mood. In fact, a lot of us are here because there was some music playing in the background that played a major role in our conception. "How?", you ask. It did so by the atmosphere it created. There is music to celebrate by, to mourn by, music for all occasions. Up music, down music, media tickertape that makes you think of the news. Traditional, contemporary, jazz, country, reggae, rap, heavy metal, rock, rhythm and blues, blues, However you desire to feel, there's some music that can help you feel it by what it does to the atmosphere. The Lord himself used music for war and battle:

And when he had consulted with the people, he appointed singers unto the LORD, and that should praise the beauty of holiness, as they went out before the army, and to say, Praise the LORD; for his mercy endureth for ever. And when they began to sing and to praise, the LORD set ambushments against the children of Ammon, Moab, and Mount Seir, which were come against Judah; and they were smitten.

2 Chronicles 20:21-22

Even the Indians picked up on this one. And kids today, when they play cowboys and Indians ... well some of you remember "Cowboys and Indians", we had that sound going! We still pull in a "sound" today! There's even a song for the bride's entrance at the wedding. We hear it and we know what's about to happen. Gabriel blows his horn with meaning! Does it not make sense then that when we praise the Lord, music is used to create the atmosphere of praise unlike anything else. Music also sets the atmosphere for the saved and unsaved, believer and non-believer to hear the Word of God. The "beast" in all of us has become soothed through the music and we are more at peace with much more obedience to sit and listen to the word of God and are even prepared for the conviction that it brings! Thus, once we have been open to conviction, we then know that change in inevitable, the Word has been received, we have had a good time and the non-believer accepts the Lord, Jesus Christ as their personal Savior. That would be the ideal service.

Again, we know that the Scriptures record that there were many times the Levites had more the heart of God than even the Priests. It is at these times that music is also used to minister even unto the Lord. For it was also the Levites that ushered in the glory cloud. This is a subject matter we often hear preached, but, fail to attach the significance of the fact that it was the Levites who were ministering and not the priests. In fact, the Scriptures record that the priests could not minister even if they wanted to at that time. They could not "stand" to minister!

It came even to pass, as the trumpeters and singers were as one, to make one sound to be heard in praising and thanking the LORD; and when they lifted up their voice with the trumpets and cymbals and instruments of music, and praised the LORD, saying, For he is good; for his mercy endureth for ever: that then the house was filled with a cloud, even the house of the LORD; So that the priests could not stand to minister by reason of the cloud: for the glory of the LORD had filled the house of God.

2 Chronicles 5:13-14

So you see, it is not like the pastor was preaching and just tearing it up and the Holy Ghost just came in and filled the place! No, not at all. Also, note in those days they were already standing, for there were no seats in the temple - which means that they had to get down on their knees because the cloud, the glory of the Lord had come in to the temple. Now you KNOW that was an awesome service! How many of THOSE types of services have you attended recently?

Additionally, we know that in several instances when the spirit of Lord made visitation, it was exemplified by way of "a cloud". Thus, the preceding only adds credence to the fact that in many places the Levites have not been given the opportunities to usher in the presence of God today as they were given in past times. Shouldn't we all get back to these principles and styles or orders of worship that we may become mightier Fishers of men...and women?

Now, not to get carried away or begin thinking that you just choose a side. Let us reiterate for clarity. There is but one head in the physical church, and that is the pastor. The pastor is the covering, angel of the house. And this does include the Music Department. Ultimately (again) the final decision as to how the service is allowed to flow is up to him or her. But let's all be open to the Spirit! The Spirit of God that will lead us in truth! There is a strange thing about the "truth." The Bible declares "the truth will set you free" it does not say that you will like it [the truth]! Can you handle the truth?

We duly note that many times there are the personal hang ups, issues, egos, etc. that prevent the Priest (or pastor) of today from being able to yield to the minister of music and vice versa when the musician feels that he or she is the "star" of the church. This may also be because of the personal hang ups, issues, ego, etc. of the minister of music or member of the music department. For this cause, a closer relationship is not only warranted but mandated, that these issues, egos, and/or hang ups are not rooted or even transcended into the services. Many times, esteem and insecurity issues are the problems with the pastor. Perhaps from feeling that he or she has to compete with the popularity of the music. If THAT be the case, "Get it together, Pastah!" For consideration and to the pastors' defense, we also recognize that sometimes the pastor cannot allow the musician or Levites to go forward for other personal reasons. This literary offering is not dealing with that specifically, just acknowledging that there are times when that is the case. I recall once seeing the musician arrive late to service, taking his time getting to the organ even after entering the sanctuary and then playing noticeably off, crazy, and loud. Extra loud! The pastor then gestured that he get up from the organ and sit "over there." Well, instead of following those directions and sitting "over there" he left out of the side door in plain view of everyone. Now, surely this was distracting. But the pastor had to also stand his ground in this matter lest the church saw him as a "wimp!" And for the sake of repair to all, the following week the musician made the apology to the pastor and the entire church.

With continuous meetings, gatherings, communication between the departments then, pastors end up with a more hands-on approach as to what the music department, its headship (which ought to be the pastor), and body is doing, simultaneously giving the music department an opportunity to enhance the vision of the house as articulated by the pastor. Music department moves (functions decisions, changes, adjustments, etc.) really ought not be surprising to pastors and we are certainly not saying that the music department should be "micromanaged" by the pastor. Although pastors may make moves that are surprising to the music minister as well as to many other auxiliaries of the church. Both, in their unified spiritual efforts still realize who the head is, just as in a marriage where the Lord has placed the husband as head of the wife, yet they both give each other submissions.

Giving thanks always for all things unto God and the Father in the name of our Lord Jesus Christ; Submitting yourselves one to another in the fear of God.
- Ephesians 5:20, 21

There is never a "tie", because the husband is the head, as is the pastor. So, the pastor is over the musician and there may be a time, Brother/Sister Pastor when you may have to submit to the better idea for the cause of the ministry as a whole even when it's NOT your idea just like you do at the house!

To the laymen however, the ultimate spirit in such a situation, ought to be one of just "making it happen" within the direction that the pastor has chosen. The focus ought not to be who gets the credit or the honor or glory. Allow God to get the glory and you will be blessed. The Holy Spirit will reward the unified spiritual efforts. It is the word!

DANGER IN THE HOUSE! CAN'T WE ALL JUST GET ALONG?

"I'm the star!" Oh, really? Well, the obvious example of this mentality is the ambition of Lucifer. The conniving ways and thoughts, operating underhandedly, etc. Do these tactics still exist in the church today? Absolutely! No doubt about it! It is no doubt that music has become a very eye-catching part of attending the church worship service today. Coupled with its commercial successes and those who participate in that area of ministry as mentioned earlier, several of the musicians and singers are indeed popular in their own right. Many have their own music careers, recordings, and following. Some are even CEOs of some very successful musical entities. Do they have covering? Well? The point is in respecting the necessity of excellence in relationship between the two departments. It is definitely the music minister who must understand the structure of the Lord when one feels that popularity reigns over position. The Lord does not care about your popularity! And yes, once again pulpiteers many times must bite the bullet, grit the teeth, lower the ego and acknowledge and respect the talent, the gift, the input of the musician/singer/Levite. Many of them are really sincere about what they do. However, the effect of power is not handled in the same way by all and is handled in a Godly manner by few. So, a sense of being "on guard" remains on both sides. Not in a paranoid way, but just because of awareness of history and the fact that the devil still

DOES exist. And know the power struggle if it ever feels that way, is not necessarily personal between the two. It's the very Jesus/Peter experience repeating itself between the two. It wasn't really about Peter. Jesus looked to Peter, but, actually spoke to Satan!

But he turned, and said unto Peter, Get thee behind me, Satan: thou art an offence unto me: for thou savourest not the things that be of God, but those that be of men.
- Matthew 16:23

Recognize. It's not that the pastor or the musician is the devil. But DO know that the devil is lurking, seeking whom he may devour and we know he loves destroying relationships. Divide and conquer is surely his way and a strong device it is. Particularly when he knows that the strength from the relationship will aid in increasing the Body of Christ, the Kingdom of God. Don't forget, he, too, is yet building his own kingdom.

When the two offices operate in covenant it will include honesty, integrity, and a communication line that whether the two agree or not they will operate with the understanding of at least agreeing to disagree. That alone will keep them moving forward. Jealousy kicks in and ruins the atmosphere and potency of the positive atmosphere when one feels more important than the other or more valuable, more wonderful, more loved, or more admired, etc. without the realization of how the unit works together in all situations (like a marriage) as this is the desire of the Lord as Paul gives us to know... Remember, the body has many members, but they work together for the good of the body. Therefore, whose idea it was becomes irrelevant! If the musician brought it to the pastor or the pastor took it to the musician, let the body be fortified and edified by the experience and God be glorified. When one part of that body begins to feel its beautified of its own... Problems! I've seen this, too. There was a musician who literally boasted to everyone he could that he was the solely responsible for the growth of this particular church. The pastor seemed to be able to do nothing or little about it because the musician was a "star"! One who traveled extensively and had audiences everywhere and would often declare his position to those audiences. However the pastor DID get the strength to sit him down and discuss the matter. The "star" chose to leave the church to "show them", believing that he could go somewhere else and be welcomed. Well, needless to say, it took years before another church would even take a chance because the word was out! Not only was he not able to quickly secure another position as Minister of Music, but his recording career also went south. Do not do it! It's <u>not</u> about you!

DON'T' THINK HE'S UGLY!

Lucifer was NOT ugly, visually, but he sure did some ugly things! Beware! Though he's filled with diverse talents, he can even preach, but, the TRUTH ain't in him! He knows this music department and does not want to see unity with this department he still feels is his. He does not want to see the unity between it and the office that preaches the Word of God! Music he was, literally. And he felt he was "the bomb" and deserved more attention. That has not changed at all!

Moreover the word of the LORD came unto me, saying, Son of man, take up a lamentation upon the king of Tyrus, and say unto him, Thus saith the Lord GOD; Thou sealest up the sum, full of wisdom, and perfect in beauty. Thou hast been in Eden the garden of God; every precious stone was thy covering, the sardius, topaz, and the diamond, the beryl, the onyx, and the jasper, the sapphire, the emerald, and the carbuncle, and gold: the workmanship of thy tablets and of thy pipes was prepared in thee in the day that thou wast created. Thou art the anointed cherub that covereth; and I have set thee so: thou wast upon the holy mountain of God; thou hast walked up and down in the midst of the stones of fire. Thou wast perfect in thy ways from the day that thou wast created, till iniquity was found in thee. By the multitude of thy merchandise they have filled the midst of thee with violence, and thou hast sinned: therefore I will cast thee as profane out of the mountain of God: and I will destroy

thee, O covering cherub, from the midst of the stones of fire. Thine heart was lifted up because of thy beauty, thou hast corrupted thy wisdom by reason of thy brightness: I will cast thee to the ground, I will lay thee before kings, that they may behold thee. Thou hast defiled thy sanctuaries by the multitude of thine iniquities, by the iniquity of thy traffick; therefore will I bring forth a fire from the midst of thee, it shall devour thee, and I will bring thee to ashes upon the earth in the sight of all them that behold thee. All they that know thee among the people shall be astonished at thee: thou shalt be a terror, and never shalt thou be any more. - Ezekiel 28:11-19

"The workmanship of the tablets and of the pipes was prepared in the day that thou was created." Lucifer had the ability to play himself! No doubt, he felt very powerful and because of this, yet denied the source of the power and the structure set before him. And just like in other area of life, he knows how to conform himself to just what you like. That thing that will surely get your attention that you be DISTRACTED from the task and direction before you. **Distractions are hindrances.** Noah's Ark only had one window and it was above! Perhaps so that no one would be distracted by what was on the side, in front, or behind. No matter the talent and ability to move the congregation, no matter the charisma, the finesse, etc, the pastor is the pastor and the musician is a help to the pastor. They complement one another for sure, but know that there is no intention here to diminish the role of the pastor or to smack the hand of the musician, for there are times when the persons occupying both positions need a hand smack! But, again, structurally, the pastor is the physical head. In the words of the great poet, Rodney King, "Can't we all just get along?"

Because of the strong value of the sacred music as well as the necessity of the Word of God, the work of Christ preached to His people. How does faith come? How is it increased? By the Word of God! And so the song that says, "Don't need a preacher!" is a lie.

How then shall they call on him in whom they have not believed? and how shall they believe in him of whom they have not heard? and how shall they hear without a preacher? And how shall they preach, except they be sent? As it is written, How

beautiful are the feet of them that preach the gospel of peace, and bring glad tidings of good things! But they have not all obeyed the gospel. For Esaias saith, Lord, who hath believed our report? So, then, faith cometh by hearing, and hearing by the Word of God. - Romans 10:14-17

What an honor to assist in the process of preparation for hearing of the Word of God! Of course, this is a process in which the devil does not want to musician to aid. Therefore, it is absolutely imperative that the empty space between the two departments come together leading the way in relationship example to the congregation in working together. There must be an open line of communication, complete with conflict resolution apparatus. Not implying that the Lord and Lucifer did not have communication, but there was disobedience and irreverence. Let's not repeat the example set before us. Because of Lucifer's actions, he was kicked out! The same it should be in this day. If there were disobedience, trouble making, discord, etc. that would be absolutely necessary! Are we talking being kicked out of the church? No, and, depending on the ministry, that certainly opens up a can of worms! Accountability and respect are important components. Chastisement comes with love. *"For whom the Lord loveth, he chasteneth…" (Hebrews 12:6a)* — There ought not be any disagreement that two Christians can not come together and reason. That is covered in the Word, too. Now asking one to leave the church would be another book, not written at this time nor by this author. However the bible does state that *"If it be possible, as much as lieth in you, live peaceably with all men." (Romans 12:8)* Apparently, sometimes it just may not be possible. Maintaining this relationship and communication helps us mortals to keep tabs on our direction and stay unified and focused. For our job is to win souls for the kingdom of God. To this end, we must be on the same team with the common goal in mind. Not to show boat. Anything contrary to the Lord's side is of the Devil, Lucifer, Satan, evil, simply NOT of God. When any part of the body begins to differ from that common goal, not assisting with the vision of the pastor, and becomes a participant of divisive measures, perpetuating disobedience and discord, he or she is jumped the bridge and taken a tunnel, a dark path that leads to destruction and the pastor's job or any leaders job is to point that out!

Now I beseech you, brethren, mark them which cause divisions and offences contrary to the doctrine which ye have learned; and avoid them. For they that are such serve not our Lord Jesus Christ, but their own belly; and by good words and fair speeches deceive the hearts of the simple.
- Romans 16:17,18

There was a musician and a pastor on one of the court TV shows. This was wrong in the first place, however, the pastor seemingly had no choice but to purse the matter. Now he didn't have to do it on national TV to show the "world" discord of the church. The musician in this case had wrecked the pastor's car and left the car at a neighbor's. The musician felt no obligation financially and further stated on national TV that HE was responsible for the growth of the pastor's church and that without him or any other musician his church would fail. He went on to state that, "These pastors need to know that it's us musicians that fill their churches!" WOW! What a statement. The judge looked at him like he was Lucifer! Though he was a young musician, and I must say I KNEW him! He had played at MY church and I knew he didn't know hymns. But this attitude is quite prevalent. And so... it became all about the money. He went on and said as he looked to the pastor, "if you were paying me right like you were supposed to..." until the judge cut him off. He implied that whatever the damage to car was not less than what was owed him so he felt no need or responsibility to pay for the damage. YET, he just left the car where it was and did not return to the church. In fact the pastor found out where the car was through a neighbor/church member. As if that weren't enough, it turns out that the musician said that he was at the neighbor's house holding a Bible Study session at FOUR O'CLOCK in the morning! Needless to say the judge and everybody in attendance cracked up and the show went to commercial! Everybody knew that this brother just was NOT right! We pray that he has learned of his incorrectness and has been restored to the Body of Christ. There are many that are in need of restoration. Restoration is also very much a part of bridging this gap! And, in order for restoration to occur, egos have to get out of the way.

DISTRIBUTIVE DUTIES

As with the ministry of those involved in the "Gospel Music Recording Industry", every participant in the making or design of any product or performance, all the way through its execution has a role, responsibility and a duty. No one is along for the free ride... well, you know. This includes all players, musicians, singers, even sound technicians, and other technicians, from stage hands, to lighting and other technicians. Even then, all around folk that assist with the "go-getting," they, too, are important in and significant to the operation. It is really imperative that we get the understanding of the importance that all who are professed Christians in our work of ministry be and exemplify just that. Be Christians. Profess and live salvation. Be bonafide members of the Kingdom of God. Certainly, we know it is not always possible nor can it even be legal in all aspects, but it is always, always a great time of ministry when all are in the flow of the Holy Spirit. Those that are around and who are not Christians will feel this and may want some. It's a time of seed planting that someone else may come with water and allow God to give the increase. It is fair and understandable, however, for leadership to seek this particularly when/if we're talking about within the confines of the church. In the church, as pastor, leader, musician, I CAN ask you if you are saved. Then too... some say they are and.............well? That is why God searches the heart. The plan of salvation (Romans 10:9) includes "believing in your heart." It is not a mere lip service thing. Imagine if the work were being distributed within these two departments with this prerequisite that we often assume, more than half of the work is already done and we're just going for results! The fact of the matter is, we go through developmental stages, creative and otherwise, and then we turn over anointed work, a complete work, to the hands of those outside of the Kingdom and expect the results that we envisioned. This is nearly impossible, even though we continuously get a foretaste of what it could really be. We never really see the fullness because of the bacteria that we have allowed to be a part of the product or the service playing a key role. Therefore, the product is not all it could be. It did not line up with the way leadership saw it, and it WAS from God. Don't doubt that. It's just that many times we entrusted the mission to diseased players. Rough, huh? I know. Growth has been stunted, effect is not what it could be. "Gift coming without repentance" is not applicable here, that would be taking that scripture out of context. We all have issues that we ought to be working on, praying for, seeking the Lord, etc. Some are doing just that. Some aren't! Some have no profession of Christianity for real and avoid the subject with the attitude that "it's none of their business!" And it is! Because their uncleanness and omission of at least repentance causes effect of the whole body. Some stand on their own statement of, "That's just how I am." And THAT is not acceptable. If this is you, maybe you need to change! Or rather, you need BE changed!

Therefore, if any man be in Christ, he is a new creature: old things are passed away; behold, all things are become new. And all things are of God, who hath reconciled us to himself by Jesus Christ, and hath given to us the ministry of reconciliation.

- Corinthians 5:17, 18

Another reason perhaps we don't get the fullness of the experience or the outcome we often crave in the worship service is if there is a malfunction in the relationship between the leadership heads. If so, it will show! The dark side, the enemy, Satan, has his plan too. We, in turn, facilitate his plan by allowing him to participate in the service and on the project through whatever area we have "a space". As far as the recording industry goes; if we [Saints of God] are the writers, producers, recorders, musicians, etc., and are not the technicians, manufacturers, distributors, then we have, in fact, allowed bacteria in to the process. The bacteria distorts the view. Yes, we are tricked into believing certain things are successful based on someone else's idea of success. It's about winning souls in to the kingdom of God! Added souls is indisputable success. Strength and unity between the two departments will give added power, strength, and might to do just that! We invite defeat of the fullness by allowing the bacteria! The fullness will not happen as long as there is bacteria in the project, event, service, etc. Does it seem impossible? Perhaps, but I say once again, this ought to provoke us to think at a higher level with higher requirements of ourselves, whereby we make an attempt to include more Builders of the Kingdom of God into our projects, services, etc. That we become more cognizant of who was actually a part of the "prayer circle" and who was not. Specifically, we turn the work over of those who were to those who were not. Well, it just doesn't make sense

that we should expect anymore than we get. The enemy (particularly when involved) is not going to take responsibility for disseminating the "Word of God", in song or otherwise.

So, even in the church, the same certainly holds true. It can no longer be a thing where we allow and make exceptions for talent over confession! Take the lesser talent and allow the Holy Spirit to do the rest by faith. We take a chance, a very bad chance when we prefer talent and never even seek to hear the testimony, the confession, the belief, the desire to do the will of the Lord. But, because he or she can sing, can play, or has an awesome gift of administration, we say "the job is yours". We have to be provoked to consider the question, "Are we inviting bacteria into responsible/leadership areas? These areas are responsible for disseminating the truth, protection the truth, and certainly telling the truth. For if this is tampered with and the truth not be told, or goes forward with bacteria (and that wouldn't be the truth), then we risk the "people not being really free." For the "truth shall set you free" ... and he who the Son sets free is free in deed". Anyone not in line with Galatians 5:22 cannot be entrusted to promote and enhance the Kingdom building process! Some are quite honest where they are. Talented or not. I remember the late Phyllis Hyman being in the house at The Center Of Hope Church in Oakland, CA, where Ernestine Cleveland Reems, (now Bishop E. C. Reems-Dickerson) is pastor. Bishop Reems acknowledged Miss Phyllis, who was truly a singer, and called her up for a solo. Miss Phyllis respectfully declined stating that she did not know any of "those" songs and did not want to be hypocritical. Consequently, Miss Phyllis instead sent up one of her background singers who was obviously very familiar and at home in church. Now while many used this as an opportunity to judge Miss Phyllis, she was actually operating in more truth than some of the members in the choir who sing anyway just because they can, but with no conviction. That conviction coupled with that anointing will make the difference in performing any duties of ministry.

WE'VE GOT GUESTS COMING!

And so we've got guests coming for the celebration. Now what? Well, that, too, brings about another situation when it comes to bettering the relationship between the two departments. Particularly when there are musical guests involved. In most cases it is the music department, minister of music, etc. who makes contact with an artist either because of special pastoral request or because his or her duty allows them the opportunity to secure whoever they deem will fit in with what is occurring. And when the latter is the case, the music minister ought to consider just that! Who's best for that time of ministry, not who is my friend and I want to book them or do their record company a favor. This is not the time! Be it traditional, contemporary, hip hop, quartet, or whatever. The artist involved needs to be as sensitive and appreciative for the invitation as the ministry involved should be sensitive and appreciative that the artist is available to accept the invitation. The level of respect has got to work both ways. Now, however, since in fact the office of the pastorate is the headship of the church, there has got to be reverence for the position, the sanctuary and the service, even if the engagement is not held at the church edifice. Whatever the venue, there is a transformation when the artist's invitation is from that of a ministry, represented with a pastor. Of course, where the spirit of the Lord IS, there IS liberty! Thus, this becomes an opportunity for the artist to dispel the bad rap that many artists have given ALL artists. The attitudes, the punctuality, the lack of reverence, the knowledge of ministry, the "do's and don'ts" of church/ministry and etiquette, etc. (here) are all under the microscope at times like these. In some cases, there's an opportunity to minister even to the headship of the church/ministry with respect to what the relationship ought to be or not. Being late and inaccessible, insensitive, over- demanding, acting like a "rock star" is not the way to assist in the kingdom building process. Even if the ministry has its own shortcomings, the musicianship must take an active role in assisting to build up the whole thing. Here's an opportunity for the "guest musical artist" to assist his or her brother in the struggle of making it better for the music department! Not help tear it down. Great, educated, talented minds come together to build. An idiot can tear it down! If it is missing a few things and not exactly "up to par" this is NOT the time to beat them down! Make suggestions, don't tear down the place with criticisms and judgments. After all, your ministry started somewhere too. And you never know what this ministry is going to turn out to be as far as being able to assist in your musical career. No matter what the shape of it. You never know who's who or what relationships people with in it may have. Just be nice. It's a time to minister! To serve!

One of the greatest organists of our time, unbeknownst perhaps to too many, is Brother Joel Bryant of Philadelphia, PA. Joel has played for everyone from the Stylistics (don't try it!) to Jennifer Holliday to Tramaine Hawkins. He is fabulous and we call him a walking encyclopedia. Anyway, Joel closes out his emails with this reminder that "ministry" and "service" are synonyms! Thought I'd pass that on to you. And at the same time, you never know what the artist's career may turn out to be in order to assist in promoting the excellence or not that's going on in your ministry. Once again, the two must work together in order to display the unified body of Christ and work it out! And we well know attitudes, insensitivity, and drama don't help to work it out! Don't get mad yet, keep reading! There are too many instances where artists come in and act like they're in a secular situation and one perhaps that they've never really been in, just "acting." That's not to belittle or shine the wrong light on the secular opportunities or environments, however, because the painful truth of that matter is that there are many secular situations and opportunities that are operated in a more Christ-like manner than some churches operate. In fact, several operate with more truth than some ministries. Once again, you just must represent and be a help to unite the body of Christ, be an example and not assist in the devil's tactics to further divide. Don't forget when it comes to the issues of music, he's all too familiar and he KNOWS how to get it done. Something little to you can be big to someone else and vice versa.

Now, this is NO excuse for contracts or agreement letters not to be followed! It is all a part of extending an invitation. Be prepared to show the hospitality! And yes, while the artist ought to show appreciation for the invitation and the hospitality, you can't just switch up on the agreement with out communication, that wouldn't be love!

Be kindly affectioned one to another with brotherly love; in honour preferring one another; Not slothful in business; fervent in spirit; serving the Lord; Rejoicing in hope; patient in tribulation; continuing instant in prayer; Distributing to the necessity of saints; given to hospitality.

- Romans 12:10-13

There must be communication. An artist arriving expecting to a piano or an organ and doesn't see it, because someone decided to go another way and secure a keyboard is not acceptable with out discussion and agreement... in writing. Getting picked up in someone's momma's car with the car seat and fast food wrappers in it when the contract stated "A-1 First Class transportation or Limo" is not acceptable without discussion and agreement in writing. When one goes away from what has been agreed upon without discussion and agreement, one CAN in fact get attitude! Attitude from the arriving camp: the artist, the musician (s), the Road Manager, etc. That's just not fair. Not fair because the purchasing party still expects the professional presentation and then some! We all ought to honor what we have signed and agreed to. We may not get all that we want, but if we at least agree to what's available and what its going to be, we'll be in a better place. BEWARE, the pastor, the pulpit is watching or getting whiff of all of this! Be thoughtful and sensitive.

At one convention there was an artist who was given the amount of time allotted and just plain ignored the ministry's outline of time. Determined to do more, cause she was "feeling it," and "didn't want to be rushed." Making statements like, "I'm just going to take my time anyway," is out of order. And yes, in this case the ministry was on time and had a timeline established, great hotel, great equipment, great transportation, just a great event. Can you imagine what the various "preachers" (the pastors of the various pulpits) were thinking? When the artist has been given an outline of time, the schedule, etc.,

it must be adhered to. Contractually and otherwise, you, as an artist, are an invited guest. Be grateful. You don't come to someone's house and tell them what to do. That's not how you represent and it is certainly not how you get invited back or anywhere else once the word is out as to how you carried on. Another instance where the artist comes in to a mega-ministry situation known for its royal treatment of everyone and they just go ALL out berserk! Once again, given the time outline, and ignores it. And, in this case, the allotted time was more than enough for most. We're talking 90 minutes. Given NINETY minutes and you TAKE 2 HOURS and only sing FOUR songs?! Now who's coming back to hear THAT again? Particularly when there was no unity with the presentation. Yes, sometimes the Spirit dictates going another direction, not singing what you were going to sing, changing the set list, giving one of the background singers an opportunity to minister a bit, all the way down to "giving the drummer some!" but you've got to be sensitive to your audience as well whether they paid a ticket or not and acknowledge the leadership of the ministry. The ministry thought enough of you to allow you to minister to the people for whom they are responsible. These are nothing short of acts of selfishness that are unacceptable and do absolutely nothing to assist in bridging the gap between the music department and the pulpit. In fact, these kinds of negative situations put more distance between the two. How and why? Ultimately, in instances like the above, the pastor (particularly a very traditional one who was reluctant in the first place) will use the situation as an "I told you so" opportunity and won't be open to allow another musical guest opportunity. THAT becomes unfair to the entire body, but is a result of someone's ego. There are times when that kind of behavior also leads to more expenses as well. However, the pastor/leadership must also recognize that not all musicians, singers, artist act or perform alike. And all should not suffer because of the ignorance of one, or some. This is not the context of Scripture with respect to the body suffering to reign with Christ! THAT Scripture as with many has been so misconstrued, it's a shame. KNOW The Word! Unfortunately, it was at a musical where I heard the preacher say that some are suffering to reign with Christ by way of their credit card debt! WHAT? You have credit card debt because you couldn't control your spending habits! That has nothing to do with your reign with Christ as far as that Scripture goes. Anyhow, so there are many opportunities for the artist as well as ministry leaders to assist in bridging the gap.

In all thy getting, get understanding will help us all. Understand contracts. Get help to do so. Be thorough. Ask questions. Be honest. If you don't know, ask! Wisdom and understanding, both are wonderful things!

Wisdom is the principal thing; therefore get wisdom: and with all thy getting get understanding. Exalt her, and she shall promote thee: she shall bring thee to honour, when thou dost embrace her. She shall give to thine head an ornament of grace: a crown of glory shall she deliver to thee.

- Proverbs 4:7-9

If it is over your head, admit it and try it again another time when you've gotten a bit more experience or resource. Don't make the ministry look bad. Get the house together before the guests come! Too many people try and do a rush job and clean the house because they know they're having guest for the weekend. Well, my mom would always say if we would keep the house clean, then we don't have to clean it up because guests are coming. Shape up the ship before the invites go out. Why allow the guest to enjoy what you don't enjoy yourself! Train our people that they, too, may have an understanding of what it all involves. For instance if your church is one that doesn't sell tickets then the people need to know the importance, sincerity, and necessity of the offering. And even so, if there are tickets, people need to understand how that works too. They need to know they need to purchase their tickets in advance and urge others to do so too. Giving on both parts is important. People need to know that the airlines and other modes of transportation cost money! When it comes to the hotels... they cost too. You've got to pay to stay! It's all relevant! Even if you're calling it a benefit. There are still expenses! Advertising costs. There are cost involved with everything from lights to sound to ticket printing to gasoline fort the vehicles that transport, grapes for the green room, juice, tea, coffee... everything! And the offering, be it by ticket or free will offering makes it happen. Now on a lighter side, think of how encouraged, motivated, and inspired the ministry, artist, and congregation are when things just go well in representation of the Body of Christ working together with out a hitch! That becomes more and more reflective of the way the operation ought to be. Christ-like! It also helps the pulpit to have trust and confidence in the operations of the music department and additionally, the music department is in a better posture to do it again. There is no question that the body of Christ needs to be more appreciative of all the talents involved. It goes back to the body having many members.

EQUIPPING THE SAINTS

Much like anything else, in order to accomplish the task at hand, those involved in the task must be equipped to do so. Spiritually, mentally, physically, emotionally, and, yes, financially. Let's deal with the financial aspect, i.e., the money. What about the money? The church gets quiet when you talk about money. Those are the non-givers. Be clear, I have not said, nor am I suggesting that there should be NO money. Nor, have I said there should be money. Many times, it simply depends on what the ministry can or cannot do. Money often causes lots of arguments and creates lots of frustration. There is nothing wrong with money! IT is not evil, it is simply the love of money that is the root of all evil.

For the love of money is the root of all evil: which while some coveted after, they have erred from the faith, and pierced themselves through with many sorrows.
I Timothy 6:10

No one's gift should be taken for granted or taken advantage of. If it's there, you ought to share! Ministry must be first and foremost - always! Just as ministry cannot be forgotten in the church, the relationship between the pastor and the musician ought not become just a financial situation…i.e., a total business matter, as in "I'll only play or participate as long as the check is there!" Likewise, whatever one gets should not be based on what someone else gets. Remember the laborers in the vineyard? Know YOUR deal! Not the deal of others! THAT cannot be your concern.

> **For the kingdom of heaven is like unto a man *that is* a householder, which went out early in the morning to hire labourers into his vineyard. And when he had agreed with the labourers for a penny a day, he sent them into his vineyard.**
>
> **- Matthew 20:1,2**

The Bible teaches us in Luke 10:7 that "the laborer is worth of his hire." In that same passage we are admonished "not to go from house to house." Certainly, this confirms that we must learn to work together and work things out, not just cut and run when things are not going as we think they should.

In all settings, respect for various vocations is a must, but this is especially true in the church world. Often times, the level of respect extended varies dependent upon the individual to whom it is being directed. If it is a rule it is a rule. If we stand when the pastor or the preacher enters, then that is what we do whether it is someone of great notoriety or not. For the Lord has anointed them all to preach the Gospel. Respect the position. You may not like the person, but the person has the position and you must give honor where honor is due. One day it could be you. When the President of the United States enters we stand and give him honor, we prepare the place and decorate and go all out. Make the presentation the best it can be no matter who it is. Do it as unto the Lord with your best and it will be great for everyone. More often than not, the necessities relative to these vocations are not understood or appreciated until times of crises. It is clearly understood that the pastor wants to sound the best he can with the equipment that is available. Churches will spend thousands of dollars for a sound system that accommodates the pulpit, but does not accommodate the music ministry (i.e., uni-directional vs. omni-directional microphones). The preacher receives the quality output and his or her voice soars as if he/she were actors Charlton Hesston, Ossie Davis, James Earl Jones or actresses Tonea Stewart or Ruby Dee. Meanwhile, the music department's ministry struggles and/or fails to deliver a quality sound and presentation. Keyboards, drums, percussion or other equipment is simply not given the same level of priority in the the ministry. Understandably, for some, this often translates to what "THEY" do is not ministry while what "I" do is the epitome of ministry. Each must respect the validity and sincerity of the other's participation in ministry. All saints must be equipped in order to do their job well.

Rev. Quincy Fielding, Jr. a former James Cleveland Singer, pastor and composer of many phenomenal songs such as "What Shall I Do" recorded by the late Rev. James Cleveland as well as by Tramaine Hawkins, also did a song, "Equipping The Saints," inspired by a passage from Ephesians which remains unforgettable to me:

And he gave some, apostles; and some, prophets; and some, evangelists; and some, pastors and teachers. <u>For the perfecting of the saints, for the work of the ministry, for the edifying of the body of Christ.</u>

-Ephesians 4:11, 12

We must equip the saints!" We must be equipped in order to do our task... even Moses was given a staff! This includes having the best equipment that there is to offer. We understand that affordability is a consideration as well. However, in many cases, affordability is inarguable when members of the music department witness extravagance heaped upon extravagance in areas of operation outside of theirs. For example, clergy men and women often boast of the cost of items such as robes, other garments, trips, furniture, the new carpeting, office machinery, cars, etc., in the presence of the members of the music department who are suffering from lack. The piano hasn't been tuned or polished while expensive lavalieres have been purchased for the clergy/pulpit and the drummer has been hoping for microphones. Monitors are placed in the pulpit, [let's say FOUR of them], so the minister really sounds good to himself or herself. Simultaneously, there is NO monitor for the keyboard player, the drummer, or even the choir soloist. All of these laborers are screaming on the inside for some attention that will enable them to display excellence in what they do, too, not to mention the fact that better working conditions would help them to experience growth in their ministry as well. In the absence of such support, encouragement or motivation, these laborers become bored and disenchanted, which means they are unable to contribute and serve the congregation as they would be otherwise. Keep in mind that some members of the music ministry are already considered professionals in their field based on their experience and they are trying to bring their constituency in to the church too! They deserve better than to be embarrassed because no thought was obviously given to the needs of the music department. Consequently, these gifted and talented laborers become "dry!" So much so that even their professional desires cause them to be inferior to others who at least come with the experience of knowing the differences in sound and blending based upon their secular and/or non-secular experiences. The failure or inability to focus on the significance of delivering high quality sounds and equipment is not limited to new, start-up ministries, this scenario occurs all too often in established churches with brand new sprawling complexes. In any case, when there is NO thought given to the music department, this type of scenario is a set up to create an atmosphere of animosity toward the pulpit and leadership. When so much detail has been given to all areas except the music ministry, there is an inherent inequity, so that the music department automatically feels less important as an entity. Speaking realistically, we understand that persons who are expert in state-of-the-art equipment may not be involved in the particular ministry which requires such expertise. It stands to reason then, that this would be the perfect time to seek expert advice, especially if the Church is building! I've been *invited* to churches with various singing aggregations and music ministries that were just beautiful! Now we were there on *invitation,* yet, we were told we could not move anything. We could make no adjustments that would have equipped the ministry to have at least a little freedom to do what they do. Yet, the ministry extending the invitation was looking for a presentation like that they had seen on the video. How could that ever happen? The saints are not equipped. Give room. Be open to adjustment. Equip the saints to do what they do!

The irony is although we fail to invest equally, we still expect our music departments to execute skillfully and sound like the recordings no matter what equipment they have or do not have to with which to work. The bottom line is, if churches just give them what they need and the church, pastor and musicians will be happy, too. Again, it need not be a power struggle. We know who the pastor is. It is only fair that we consider upgrading equipment, and do so on a continuous basis. Don't just tune the piano because it's time for the anniversary or because a special guest is coming and forget about it four months later or as needed. Then there are those times when just the wrong people are consulted with purchases. That's why it is of paramount importance to get someone who knows, i.e., someone who really knows and YOU know THEIR work and experience. Too often "board members" make decisions on issues they know nothing about and will make the higher price purchase. You ought to know a high price does NOT necessarily mean it is the best for the situation. At least allow that there be a voice for consideration. You may learn something in the process as well. Too often folk go with the cabinetry, rather than what's on the inside and never realize that the real deal is not worth it! So, then you have a speaker with a pretty cabinet and IT is no good for your situation. Or a keyboard with a pretty wood cabinet casing and there is no commensurate sound quality after you have spent thousands more than necessary and expect the musicians to use it anyway! This is simply not fair! The entire matter could have been handled and resolved with a phone call and the gap would have been bridged a little more! With all these things in mind, let there be consistency in care and concern regarding equipping the saints. Take care, take care, and clean, clean, clean! All parties ought to show gratitude and appreciation. Not only will rewards be there for all, but, you will be able to KEEP THE PEACE!

PRAISE AND WORSHIP

Unlike preaching or teaching the Word of God which is often the duty of the pastor, other ministers or deacons, the act of praise and worship is an eternal act. Our praise and worship shall last for eternity. Preaching, teaching, administration, etc. have an end. In order to help bridge the gap, the pulpit has to help the congregation, music department, and other pulpiteers to understand this. Just as we believe in giving credit where credit is due (well, some of us), so should we point out value where value is. Again, this is easy to do when ego is not the issue. Thus, the ability and/or discipline that the musical staff (some of whom might also be ministers of the Word) displays in leading the congregation in praise and worship models the type of discipline that church leaders should seek, rather than feel that he/she is so superior that they need only observe, not participate in the service.

The ability to capture the attention of the Lord has no exclusivity. In many of our churches, those in the pulpit are not present for praise and worship in the traditional Sunday morning service or any other special service where praise and worship is incorporated. It is often treated as a period of "stretching." You know, "just keep things going if we are not prepared to commence the actual body of the service." I recall being at a church to preach and the praise team was out there just going for it and I wanted to be in that number. I could hear them through the walls and there was even a TV monitor in the pastor's study. I asked if we could go out and be a part of Praise and

Worship and that pastor looked at me as if I were speaking a foreign language. One that he did not understand. But, for some, going out and participating will not allow time for gossip and other non-productive conversations. I say, get on out there, pastors and participate in that Praise and Worship! It is for everyone.

Needless to say, praise and worship ought to flow throughout the service, continuously acknowledging the Holy Spirit, the very presence of God! Moreover, when leadership adopts this attitude, it is indicative of a lack of awareness of the leader's ability to increase his/her recognition and sensitivity to the move of the Holy Spirit, His attributes, and all His powers. The bottom line in this case is that a one-ness is created through joint participation and collaboration between church leader of leadership and musician staff.

There should be no separation such as "you do your part and I'll do my part." That mindset facilitates a disjointed service and the fact that there is "no flow" shows. Having two different parts with no bridge is also exemplified when the service is "turned over to the pulpit". Of course, the pulpit has its particular charge, however, pulpit members should also be contemporaneous participants in what will soon become the ultimate eternal experience. If not, they will be lost when they discover "this is all we do!" Stated more bluntly, pulpiteers, YOUR JOB HAS AN END, the praise team's job does not!

Pulpiteers need to learn and understand praise and worship! The praise team does not need to learn to preach! It's time to get with the program! Those members of the praise team, the congregants who participate in this act, will be ready. Everyone needs to learn and understand praise and worship. It can be more effective when it is encouraged and endorsed by way of active participation from the pulpit because the congregation has a better example to follow. It will also reiterate the fact that you don't have to be an excellent singer to participate in praise and worship. Now you may not be able to LEAD it, but you can certainly participate (without a mic)!

Let me add here that the basic development of these literary thoughts occurred not only from desire, but, also from vision, belief and knowledge that if the two departments or components would understand themselves and their functions on a more broad spiritual spectrum as we are in spiritual warfare that they would better able and equipped to approach the war and conflicts from a different perspective and would also have more of a realization of their potential impact on the kingdom building process overall. Throughout my many travels and experiences, I have seen so many things that resulted from ego/power struggles and/or what I call "see me demons" that I often wonder, "Who is really concentrating on the work?" It is all still about the "work" of the ministry!

THE CHARACTERS

What does the musician do when the pastor has gone aloof? That situation is generally more difficult for the musician because when the musician has gone aloof, most pastors find an easy remedy. The question, however, is whether the musician has a right to question what is happening with the pastor when thing go awry. Does the musician have the responsibility to participate in the teaching/learning programs of the church such as Bible study, Sunday School or other programs in general? What does the musician do when it is clear that there is trouble in the camp? If you are a musician, have you ever wondered, "What do I do when I KNOW the pastor is just plain wrong? Scripturally wrong? Morally wrong? What do I do?"

If you're a pastor, and you know you're wrong...how do you face the musician who knows of your wrong doings? Remember, the Bible teaches us that "pride goeth before the fall." If we operate as true Christians and in love, this should be a time of prayer, repentance, upholding, forgiving, allowing God to manifest the victory. It can be done and most likely will be done before the people of God and they, too, will be strengthened just by being a witness of the restoration. That is, if they have the knowledge of such. If they don't know, they will be benefactors because the parties involved will be strengthened and able to go forward stronger with boldness, clarity, and freedom. The Bible also teaches:

"Brethren, if a man be overtaken in a fault, ye which are spiritual, restore such an one in the spirit of meekness; considering thyself, lest thou also be tempted."

- Galatians 6:1

We can do this. We are over comers! The emphasis here is on.. "ye which are spiritual." You'll really find out "who's who" going through this trial. So, the questions are covered, what is important to note in the answer is the word "IF." Now, what can we do about that? The victorious outcome of the matter is predicated on the "IF" factor. There is no question that there are also difficult times and situations that come along with the scenario of these offices…but…. both parties must stay strong for the sake of the ministry! There is one Minister of Music I know of who was so connected to his pastor you would have thought he was the Assistant Pastor on salary. Beyond his skillful playing of the organ and his obvious anticipation of the pastor's next move that he be ready, he was just there. Desiring to be a part of the fabric of the ministry. His name is synonymous with the church itself. If the pastor needed any help, he was right there. Even before some deacons or other officers of the church. Willing to help. He was on the front line. He loved the pastor and understood the need to be close to him and help and protect where ever he could. Though his pastor is now gone on to be with the Lord, this brother is yet blessed because of his service to him.

FROM EXPERIENCE

When asked the question, "What has been the most difficult thing for you as a Minister of Music?", World renowned singer, songwriter, arranger, producer, musician, personality personified, Grammy Award winner, father of contemporary gospel music and the founder of the Edwin Hawkins Music & Arts Seminar, Dr. Edwin Hawkins responds that his most difficult experiences were the "awkward times." He further proclaims that they also were perhaps some of the most valuable in retrospect. Whether good or bad, the fundamental import of our experiences is for us to receive life lessons. It is imperative that we learn and grow from them in order to assist the ministry.

It is also imperative that we remain planted, not distinguish ourselves as a "church hopper." Of course, there are many instances we can recall when trouble has arisen, the Minister of Music is the first to run or hide and not, in fact, face the music!" Facing the music represents an exercise in character building. Not that you're always wrong or in trouble, but as a Minister of Music you are a role model. There are men and women, boys and girls who are looking up to you. There's a standard to which you are being held and a particular level of expectation on the part of the congregation with which you may not be comfortable.

Of course you know Edwin's younger brother, the awesomely anointed author, arranger, singer, preacher, teacher, and founder of the Love Fellowship, Bishop Walter Hawkins who has penned and/or arranged such phenomenal tunes as "Changed", "Going Up Yonder" sung by Tramaine Hawkins and "Marvelous", "What Is This?' and "be Grateful", sung by Lynette Hawkins Stephens along with innumerable other hits. You cannot be in music ministry or the Gospel industry and not know these multitalented Hawkins Brothers. Bishop Walter Hawkins says the most difficult part of music ministry for him is "letting go!" It stands to reason that in this day and time there are a lot of pastors who are excellent, skilled musicians themselves. I believe this is due to the fact that many pastors are "frustrated" musicians and/or God's elevation from music ministry to the ministry of the Word could be part of His Master Plan in bridging the gap between the music department and the pulpit. These two offices should be right next door to each other or as close to each other as possible to not let anything come in between them. The two belong together like a marriage. It's no wonder that, more and more, we hear of musicians being called to preach or being called to pastor. There even seems to be a move of liberation in which you find that many pastors you've known for years were "in the closet" with their musical abilities and talents. Who knew that Rev. Jones stays in his basement recording songs he has written in his deep baritone voice! Hahahaha... it happens all the time!

Bishop Hawkins says due to his own expectations, successes, and talents, he realizes that it hard for a musician to not feel intimidated. There's a job that must be done when one is in a Bishop's position, so Bishop Hawkins would often find himself catering to the music department because they'd continuously look to him to assist unlike the other departments. Needless to say that when it is known that the pastor can do it too, they'll always look to you to do it! And, if you don't put a stop to it, letting go no matter how much you love it, the Music Department will never grow and be solid on its own. Most founding pastors, as well as musically inclined pastors can surely relate to that. Those with the humble beginnings can easily recall the time when the pastor would have to open the service, read the scripture, said the prayer, sing the song, and then preach, too. Well, the pastor who is/was also a musician can be found on the keyboard or other instrument in that scenario would play too! Those observing these talents in others and seeing how well it is done can be more than a little intimidating to the musicians regardless of whether the pastor has achieved local or national acclaim. The flip side, however, is if you are the one who isn't able to discharge music ministry well, then it is regarded as an opportunity. Surely, the pastor ought to be free to pastor, to receive from the Holy Spirit direction for himself and the ministry and should not be locked in to position in other auxiliaries of the church. This however does not mean that the pastor should not be involved. I don't believe that's what Bishop Hawkins was saying at all.

After all, when Bishop Hawkins needs singers for a project, performance, or tour, he doesn't have to look far at all! But for the ministry's sake, the musicians are charged with coming up with songs that fit the ministry, but not keep them there. Move them forward. The singers, programs, etc., that the congregation will enjoy as they grow and flow with the direction of the pastor... and flowing with the pastor IS growing! Seeking the direction and instruction of the Holy Spirit to be able to do so for the sake of the ministry and not your own self gain is also growth!

Another great musician and historian is Patrick Henderson. Known as one of our contemporary ushers of the "Praise & Worship" experience to the church. Patrick proclaims that when you get these songs of praise and worship in the hearts of the congregation they'll carry them for the rest of their lives and the word will become more natural for them to understand. I find every conversation with Patrick awesome. I would imagine that was David's thought as well. When you look at what David says in Psalm 119, it backs up this very thought. The fact that we can hold the word in our hearts in a much easier way when learned through song, through praise.

I will praise thee with uprightness of heart, when I shall have learned thy righteous judgments. 8 I will keep thy statutes: O forsake me not utterly. Wherewithal shall a young man cleanse his way? by taking heed thereto according to thy word. With my whole heart have I sought thee: O let me not wander from thy commandments. Thy word have I hid in mine heart, that I might

not sin against thee. Blessed art thou, O LORD: teach me thy statutes.

Psalm 119:7-12

We've got some great examples on the front line of ministry today leading the way in praise and worship with excellence. Kevin Bond, Stephen Hurd, Israel Houghton, Judith Christie McAllister just to name a few. Consider the list of pastors who started with singing careers and/or pastors that ended up in music ministry as well like; Donnie McClurkin, Maceo Woods, Milton Brunson, Paul Morton, T. D. Jakes, Michael Kelsey, Andre Crouch, Tonex, Andrew Ford, Charles Hayes, Shirley Caesar, Hezekiah Walker, Marvin Winans, John P. Kee, Timothy Wright, Allen Wiggins, Bruce Allen, Carlton Pearson, Beverly Crawford, Walter Hawkins, the late, great, James Cleveland, and the list goes on and on. It reveals the connection of the two areas of ministry. It reveals the two simply work together! Of course nothing replaces the Word of God, but you can't deny the power of the Word of God in song! It is no doubt that the *experiences* of these have given them the ability to minister from a different perspective with added conviction, power, authority, and of course the anointing! The experiences certainly add power to the ministry. I recall Bishop T.D. Jakes sharing with me when he learned that I was about to pastor. He told me to tape everything! Tape as much as I could and review the tapes a year or two or even three afterwards and through added experience, I'd be able to deliver the same messages with more conviction and power because of the experience. True, very true and great advice! You can't beat the experience. But you must be willing to get the lesson. Even in frustration, there's a lesson. I've learned you do have a choice. You can remain frustrated or you can do something about it! Your experience will be a plus to the ministry as the Lord leads you. Paul proclaimed himself the chief sinner, but God placed him in the ministry and used him mightily! His **experiences** (the good and bad) were not in vain as much was done in ignorance.

And I thank Christ Jesus our Lord, who hath enabled me, for that he counted me faithful, putting me into the

ministry; Who was before a blasphemer, and a perse-cutor, and injurious: but I obtained mercy, because I did it ignorantly in unbelief. And the grace of our Lord was exceeding abundant with faith and love which is in Christ Jesus.

I Timothy 1:12-14

Consider that all have experiences that could prove useful to the ministry and aid in winning souls for the Kingdom. Stop and listen to one another and bridge the gap!

WHERE DID THEY GO?

When musicians end up in other genres of music such as R & B or whatever, as opposed to the Gospel on which they were raised or as was their original intention or desire, it is often a result of the lack of opportunity to express themselves or simply be accepted as their creative selves, so they just "roll out!" They shake the dust! I'm talking about the ones who KNOW they have something to offer and are not given the opportunity. We must not forget that many of them know the Word as well.

> **"And if the house be worthy, let your peace come upon it: but if it be not worthy, let your peace return to you. And, whosoever shall not receive you, nor hear your words, when ye depart out of that house or city, shake off the dust of your feet!"**
>
> **- Matthew 10:13, 14**

The list of those who started in the church and ended up in other genres is certainly too lengthy to cover here, it would read like a telephone book. To the church's credit, we also must realize, however, that not all who left the genre had a real desire or intention to remain in the genre or even in the church in the first place. For many, the church simply served as a place of convenience used for exercising one's gift, getting exposure, practicing, learning licks, etc. Still some today, after the secular situation and stardom falls through and turns its back on them, they return to the church. YES, "The doors of the church are open!" Nothing wrong with the prodigal son aspect of the return, however, many of those particular people are still in search of or in dire need of attention, ego-stroking, and other frills that come with the former status including the preferential treatment of front row seating, the recognition of being in the house, etc. None of which is there room for in ministry! I know, I know, we do it to our own chosen ones. However you put it, when the title becomes more important than the "gig", there's trouble!

Certainly, though, there are those that have remained faithful to the genre of Gospel, Sacred, or Contemporary Christian Music. I would dare to stretch and mention that there are even many whose talents have taken them to heights unknown in other genres of music, yet their faith and their faithfulness have remained in the church. Hmmmmm. Those, too, would read like a telephone book. Get this: MUSIC is a God-given thing! Now if it tells of the good news of Jesus Christ, it is GOSPEL! Say amen, somebody! If it doesn't tell the good news, it is God-given talent being used for something other than giving God the glory and honor. Yet, we certainly are not in place to be judgmental with such artists who at least desire to be a part of the body and participate. As yet, we have issues that need attention as well so that we can cut some of the confusion. For example. I've often been asked, "What is the difference between "Contemporary Christian Music" and "Gospel Music?" What is the answer to this question supposed to be? That "one is "Black Music" and one is "White Music", but they both are about the Lord?" Now does THAT make sense? That doesn't help with the kingdom building process. It adds to division and should not be given more fuel. Let us stick to what's gospel is gospel. The good news of Jesus Christ! And that good news is for ALL!

Be mindful, too, that we are not just talking about leaving the genre of Gospel Music or the church as a whole, but just the fact that many musicians have left their local church before its time. They experienced premature cut-offs because of egos and other spirits of negativity, misunderstandings, etc. when an issue or things just didn't go their way or they were released for reasons "unknown." Some of them end up doing well and recovering from whatever the situation was when they stick to it and keep hold to God's unchanging hand. In lots of cases, however, a bruise remains and irreparable harm has been done. Some go so far as to say they're never going to another church. Lord Help! We have a saying that goes, "It's all good!" When the truth of matter is, "No, it is not all good, but we know that "all things work together FOR the good of them that love God and who are called according to His purpose. So where ever they went, let's let them know that they can come back home. They too are a soul and whatever it was that sent them out has become a testimony. Let's work it out and give God the glory! If you're one that left, find a church home and be healed by the power of God and allow him to direct you with the use of your gifts. These is a place for you in the Kingdom of God and you'll be able to help somebody else. The purpose will be revealed.

And we know that all things work together for good to them that love God, to them who are the called according to *His* purpose.

- Romans 8:28

Again, we must emphasize, without commitment, there's nothing! It is a must that all should "have a song" and your life becomes your sermon, enabling us all to be ministers. This illustrates once more, the Power of a song!

When ye come together, everyone of you hath a psalm.

- John 38:3

THE CONCLUSION

The conclusion of the whole matter as recorded in Ecclesiastes is to fear God and keep His commandments.

Let us hear the conclusion of the whole matter: Fear God, and keep his commandments: for this *is* the whole *duty* of man. 14 For God shall bring every work into judgment, with every secret thing, whether *it be* good, or whether *it be* evil.

Ecclesiastes 12:13 & 14

We have a clear mandate here! For if we recognize and agree with this need, then we ought to be provoked to immediately do what we can to make repair to this relationship and anything else we see that needs our aid that we have the ability to assist as we perpetuate excellence in ministry. For it would be sin not to aid or even try when we have been equipped to help.

Let the priests take *it* to them, every man of his acquaintance: and let them repair the breaches of the house, where so ever any breach shall be found.

II Kings 12:5

So you may ask, is this everything I need to know in order to get the job done? Most likely not, because situations vary from ministry to ministry and some things have to be tailored to fit the specific ministry. But it's a great start to any ministry! I have a member at my church, Brother Reggie Allen who has been blessed to own his own fitness training studio. He and his wife, Jackie are faithful tithers. They were also featured in the November (2005) issue of Ebony Magazine, page 192! The name of the studio is called "Mind B 4 Body Fitness Studio." The title is a message with in itself. It indeed starts with the mind. *For there first must be a willing mind!* The rest will follow. It can be done. Let's get going. We can have this!

Now therefore perform the doing *of it*; **that as** *there was* **a readiness to will, so** *there may be* **a performance also out of that which ye have. For if there be first a willing mind,** *it is* **accepted according to that a man hath,** *and* **not according to that he hath not.**

II Corinthians 8:11 & 12

At the conclusion of all of my radio broadcast I would close with the music ministry of Andrae Crouch and the song, "I'll Be Thinking Of You." A powerful song with Andrae and Krystal Murden, featuring Stevie Wonder on harmonica. It also says with in the song, "I'll be praying for you!" The intro was just enough for me to get in one of my favorite scripture passages from Philippians 4:6 & 7 *(Living Bible Translation)*

Don't worry about anything; instead, pray about everything. Tell God your needs, and don't forget to thank him for his answers. If you do this, you will experience God's peace, which is far more wonderful than the human mind can understand. His peace will keep your hearts and thoughts quiet and at rest as you trust in Christ Jesus.

PEACE!

Printed in the United States
46590LVS00004B/160

9 781597 819534